THE
ABC's
FOR
UU
NEWCOMERS

A brief introduction to Unitarian Universalism

BY WILLIAM CLEARY

LILAC MOUNTAIN BOOKS
Jericho, Vermont

First printing August 2002

Printed in the United States of America

Designed by Anne Linton

Additional copies are available from:
    Unitarian Universalist Church
    152 Pearl Street
    Burlington, VT 05401
    (802) 862-5630

ISBN 0-9709845-1-0

ACKNOWLEDGEMENTS
Excerpt on page 19 from *New Revised Standard Version Bible*, copyright 1989, Division of Christian Education of the National Council of the Churches of Christ in the United States of America; used by permission; all rights reserved. Citation on page 5 from *The Collected Poems of Langston Hughes* by Langston Hughes, copyright 1994 by The Estate of Langston Hughes; used by permission of Alfred A. Knopf, a division of Random House, Inc.. Permission requests for other quotations resulted in judgments of "fair use" and a debt of gratitude to the Unitarian Universalist Association.

Table of Contents

Subjects Covered

THIS IS AN OLD FASHIONED BOOK, an *Abecedary*, designed to carry you lightheartedly through the basics of the religion called Unitarian Universalism. The ABC's give you 26 stepping stones, and each of the stones is decorated with a rhyming couplet (which you could sing to the tune of "My Favorite Things.") By the time you get to Z, you will be ready to meet a few of the heroes and heroines of the UU movement (page 56), and perhaps you'll feel curious about how UU people might pray or meditate (page 59 and 61). How the whole project came about is explained on page 62. Welcome to a religion that opens its door to absolutely everyone in the world — and especially to You.

— William Cleary

A is for Answers, but
questions come first —
As cold drinks taste better
when you feel a thirst.

ANSWERS Thomas Jefferson gives this advice: "Question with reason even the existence of a God because, if there is one, he must more approve of the homage of reason than that of blindfolded fear."

Questions are the beginning of UU religion. Some other religions begin with answers, revelations supposedly given to human-kind long years ago. From these answers they form their creed. UUism is non-creedal. We also honor doubts. "By doubting we come to the truth," said Cicero. "Faith and doubt are the twin offspring of mystery," said John Mattuck, which sounds very Unitarian Universalist. We study our UU religion with blindfolds off and without fear, an approach that is very demanding, and requires that **we follow reason** and inspiration wherever it may lead.

This doesn't mean UUs believe nothing at all. All members are entitled to their own beliefs: some are Christian, some Jewish, some Buddhist or another tradition. Some are atheists, or may call themselves "humanists" (who come in many kinds). All are welcomed, and the diversity is rich.

But questions are primary. One very popular guidebook to UUism is *100 Questions That Non-Members Ask About Unitarian Universalism* by John Sias. In *A Chosen Faith: an Introduction to Unitarian Universalism* (Beacon 1998), one of the authors, Forrest Church — who believes in a God — says to someone who doesn't believe: "Tell me about the God you don't believe in. The chances are that I don't believe in 'him' either." Both books are excellent and available from the UUA Bookstore in Boston at (800) 215-9076.

According to denominational rankings in recent studies, the 220,000 UUs in the US are an important faith community, ranking **number one in education**. It's also a growing faith, gaining members every year for the last 20 years.

"Hold fast to dreams, for if dreams die,
Life is a broken-winged bird that cannot fly.
Hold fast to dreams for when dreams go,
Life is a barren field, frozen with snow."

LANGSTON HUGHES

UU Service Book #488

B is for **B**eauty
  and **B**lossoms and **B**liss:
The start of religion
    is awe for what is!

BEAUTY Awe is where religions all start. The beauty of spring blossoms is awesome, people are awesome, the blissful moments of life are awesome. We see the antics of a beautiful three year old and we are speechless, amazed, full of awe. How could a child be so winning, so winsome?

Shining through that child, perhaps, is **a Mystery**, something lurking there unseen in the astonishing design of the young person, in the harmonious melody of the child's qualities, not like the pile-up of colors in a compost heap but like the colorful curve of a gorgeous rainbow. Did not an intelligence bring it about? Is there some divine spirit at work: a mind, a lovingness, an inventiveness? Unitarian Universalists honor questions like these, and more sobering questions too: what of the awesome mysteries of pain and death? Is a life after death possible? Without knowing many answers, we gather to reverence the questions. That's religion. It begins in awe.

The present **headquarters of the UUA** is 25 Beacon Street, Boston, Ma 02108, (617) 742-2100, with a web address of www.uua.org.

"Whoever you are, no matter how lonely,
the world offers itself to your imagination,
calls to you like the wild geese, harsh and exciting -
over and over announcing your place in her family of
things."

MARY OLIVER
UU Service Book #490

C is for Church,
    one short hour of retreat,
But some go to synagogues,
    mosques or just meet.

CHURCH UUs meet in places of worship called by various names: churches, meeting houses, chapels, and — if they are just getting started and are lay-led without paid ministers — may meet in schools or private homes and may call themselves fellowships or societies. For UUs isolated from any nearby society there is the Church of the Larger Fellowship (CLF), a national organization with a permanent minister-leader offering religious information, support and educational material for children. Find it at **www.uua.org**. CLF's student service brings UUism to college-age youth wherever they live. Available is the monthly journal "Quest" and numerous on-line resources.

The UU meeting place may be decorated as "sacred space" but usually it looks like a rather formal meeting room. The hymn book usually contains many familiar hymns and songs, but often with the words changed to reflect our non-creedal approach.

UUism is not a church in the ordinary, Christian sense of that word. The concept of church comes from Judaism (wherein Christianity developed) in which the people felt called together by God: the Quhal Jahweh, or God's chosen people. UUs are not a church in this sense. They feel **called together, but by common sense and intuition.**

Another meaning of church is the one used above: "an hour of retreat," i.e., going to church, meeting with others to celebrate together the mysteries and challenges of life. Unitarian Universalists talk about belonging to a church, but it is more accurately called a congregation.

"The Reign of God is not coming as you hope
to catch sight of it. No one will say
'Here it is' or 'There it is,' for the Reign of God
is now in your midst. . . "

LUKE
UU Service Book #491

D is for **D**ifference
enriching our lives
Where lifestyles are many
and openness thrives.

DIFFERENCE In many religions, everyone believes the same things, everyone behaves somewhat alike, accepting the same three C's: Creed (list of beliefs), Code (what is right and wrong) and Cult (ways of worshipping together).

But UU's are **famous for their differences**, not for their sameness. The society has agreed on just seven "principles," but these basic ideas allow and encourage diversity. We are allowed to disagree on what we believe, on what is right and wrong, and on how to worship — as long as we accept what is sometimes called the UU covenant or "The Seven Commitments":

(1) the inherent worth of every person;

(2) justice and compassion as fundamental virtues;

(3) mutual respect for each other, and the promotion of spiritual growth;

(4) the free search for truth and meaning in human life;

(5) each conscience as sovereign — with group decisions reached democratically;

(6) the value of worldwide peace. liberty, and justice;

(7) reverence for the web of life.

This seven-part covenant is what we believe in: not a creed, a code or a cult. It contains our foundational ideas.

Newcomers are **not expected to change** their belief system when they join a UU community, just to make this covenant their own. They are expected to take part in church life as best they can, to help pay, if possible, the costs of maintaining services, and to be tolerant of other people and of opinions other than their own.

"And as you are patient
with our struggles to learn,
so shall we be patient
with ourselves and each other. . .
You are the embrace that heartens
And the freedom beyond fear."

STARHAWK

UU Service Book #524

E is for Equal:

    where women and men

Can listen and speak,

    and say "No!" or "Amen!"...

EQUAL Within Unitarian Universalism women and men are completely equal — while many conventional religions reflect within themselves the inequalities of the culture around them — where women are often considered second-class in thinking, second-class in virtue, and second-class humans. The UU faith claims the highest percentage of **pulpits served by women** of any mainline denomination.

Males are generally dominant everywhere in our culture, in courts, politics, banking, medicine, education and religion; they earn more money for work identical to what women do, are consulted much more than are women, and run most of the government. What women have to say is not always valued. However among UUs, women are presumed to hold the same level of gifts and abilities as do men, and many UU church leaders are — and have been since the beginning — women.

In UUism, a woman's "No" is as powerful as a man's, and her endorsement or "Amen" just as meaningful. Our denomination was the **first in the U.S.** to sanction a woman as minister, the Reverend Olympia Brown, in 1863. Unitarian Universalist women have been among the most famous in U.S. history, like Susan B. Anthony, Beatrix Potter, Amy Lowell, Julia Ward Howe, Clara Barton and Abigail Adams.

Ministry in the UU faith is similar to ministry in Jewish or Protestant denominations. The UU communities own and operate their own churches, and are responsible for choosing a minister qualified for the task.

"Never doubt that a small group of thoughtful, committed citizens can change the world; indeed it's the only thing that ever has."

MARGARET MEAD
UU Service Book #561

F is for Friendly,

the way we converse —

Without always judging

who's better or worse.

FRIENDLY All across history, people have shown themselves most un-friendly in the area of religion and belief, burning people at the stake for denying some "truth" of religion, and waging murderous wars against nations of other religious persuasions.

Today's UU Association is a kind of safe plateau where people of our culture who have opposed some things in the dominant religions and **dissented from common beliefs** can find a place of peace and agreement. For UUs, the great dissenters over the ages are their heroes and heroines, and within the UU "church" today every kind of opinion is found.

You may consider yourself Protestant or Catholic, Hindu or Buddhist, Jewish or Pagan, believer or unbeliever, and still be a good UU. The only requirement is to honor the seven fundamental UU commitments: to respect, to equality, to openness, to encouragement, to democracy, to compassion, and to earth-friendliness.

Humanism is am important movement both within and outside of UUism. Often when a UU is called a humanist, it means the person is not a believer in a god or a supernatural world, but other UUs call themselves "religious humanists" or "secular humanists." It is not an exact title but stresses concentration on human values and ethics, rather than on spirituality or religion. Within the UUA, humanists are well organized — and comfortable.

"May I be no one's enemy and may I by the friend of that which is eternal and abides. May I wish for every person's happiness and envy none. May I never rejoice in the ill fortune of one who has wronged me. May I, to the extent of my power, give needful help to all who are in want."

EUSEBIUS
UU Service Book #521

G is for "Goddess,"
        a name with a twist,
Another is "God,"
        and they both may exist.

GODDESS This is a name sometimes given, even by UUs, to the world's creator. It has a "twist" in it because the creator is usually given the name "God," a male word, like the common name "Lord." Goddess is feminine — although any creator spirit would necessarily not have a gender at all — since gender is based on bodily form and spirits would have no bodies.

It is ultimately impossible to name God adequately, but it is interesting to note that Paul of Tarsus speaking in Athens (in Acts 17:28) describes God as the one "…in whom we live and move and have our being," ascribing the words to "some of your own (non-Christian) writers." We now know that writer to have been Epimenides, a 7th century BCE Cretan poet and philosopher. That divine spirit mentioned by Paul was **metaphorically female**, of course, since the only instance of living and moving and having being within another is in human pregnancy, a female analogy.

Some UUs call themselves "pagans" and practice spiritualities and rituals that originated outside the influence of any major religion. They celebrate many of the special days that are marked by the position of cosmic bodies, and carry out the rituals of earth-centered chant and dance. Some call themselves "witches" and cultivate rituals of circles and labyrinths. **These groups are welcomed in UUism** and often find a place for their practices within or alongside a UU community.

One favorite ritual among UUs is the flaming chalice, usually lit at the start of worship. It has many significances, but seems to have been invented by the followers of the martyr of the 1400s, Jan Hus, and symbolized for them the doctrine for which Hus was put to death: offering the chalice (symbolizing equality) to lay people. The flames symbolize his manner of martyrdom, and stand primarily for liberty of mind. Others claim it originated in 1941 as a freedom symbol, used by refugees fleeing Naziism.

"I am being driven forward into an unknown land.
The pass grows steeper, the air colder and sharper.
A wind from my unknown goal stirs the strings of
expectation."

DAG HAMMARSKJOLD
UU Service Book #486

H is for **H**unger
which leads to despair!
Although food is ample,
we've not learned to share.

HUNGER This earth has plenty of food, scholars tell us, but we lack the will to distribute it so all can eat. Also, every authentic religion will urge people — partly out of gratitude that they have food themselves — to feed the hungry, give drink to the thirsty, and care for the needy. Jesus of Nazareth, for instance, based the Final Judgment on it. It is the common belief among people of faith that the human race is essentially all one family, that everyone is related to everyone else, all children of the same creation, **bound to each other**, obligated to be compassionate.

This is not new. In ancient Greek and Roman religion, a lovely story was told of Baucis and Philemon, an elderly couple full of compassion. In the story the world's chief God and his son were wandering about the earth **disguised as needy people**, taking note of how people treated them. In one village the unkind people refused them food and shelter, but two elderly people, Baucis and Philemon, invited the needy people in and gave them their best food and wine. When the wine bowl miraculously filled up again and again, the couple recognized their guests as gods. Suddenly the little house changed into a temple, and the old couple became its honored priestess and priest. Later, when they were about to die, Baucis and Philemon begged never to be separated, and the gods made them into two great trees standing side by side.

The hungry and destitute often head instinctively for a church, sensing that being compassionate goes with being religious.

"The spirit of God has sent me
to bring good news to the oppressed,
to bind up the broken hearted,
to proclaim liberty to captives
and release to prisoners,
to comfort all who mourn."

ISAIAH 61

UU Service Book #571

I is for Illness,

 which comes to us all,

And helping the sick

 is a spiritual call.

ILLNESS In early Unitarian leader, Ralph Waldo Emerson said: "We forget ourselves and our destinies in health, and the chief use of temporary sickness is to remind us of these concerns."

Illness truly reminds us that **we are not immortal**, that it is our destiny one day to die. Illness gives us something to think about deeply. Still, "it takes many to be intelligent," said Pope John XXIII — so we need other people nearby to help us be intelligent about our health, our illnesses, and our destiny.

Thus visiting the sick is considered a priority by UUs. Having a visitor when you are not feeling well is usually comforting. It also helps the visitor to experience enlightenment as well. **Every sickness**, Emerson reminds us, underlines the most important concerns of the good life.

"Grandfather, Sacred One, teach us love,
compassion, and honor that we may heal
the earth and heal each other."

OJIBWAY INDIANS
UU Service Book #518

J is for Justice,
        to share all the wealth
Of earthly resources
        and safety and health.

JUSTICE   Unitarian Universalism is committed to the ideal of justice in the world: "justice, equity and compassion in human relations" is its second principle.

Justice is a very demanding precept, and absolutely fundamental in the spirituality of every major religion and of the Bible. In the Hebrew scripture, the book of Isaiah, chapter 58, God says: "Is not this the sort of fast that pleases me — to break unjust fetters and undo the thongs of the yoke, to let the oppressed go free and break every yoke, to share your bread with the hungry, and shelter the homeless poor, to clothe the person you see to be naked, and not turn from your own kin?"

The Christian scriptures, sometimes called the New Testament, climaxes in the twenty fifth chapter of Matthew where the author has Jesus saying in effect that the poor judge the world. "Whatever you did to the least of my brethren, you did to me," says the world's judge, the Christ. Compassionate actions are priorities for many UUs. The **UU Service Committee**, headquartered in Cambridge (130 Prospect St., Cambridge, MA 02130, (617) 868-6600), devotes itself to every kind of care for those in need, and organizes work to alleviate suffering all over the world. By joining the Service Committee you can feel a part of that international effort.

Injustice can be seen in many places in our culture, where people do not enjoy their rightful share of earthly resources, education and security, and UU churches are widely known for championing these causes.

"We are caught in an inescapable network
of mutuality, tied in a single garment of destiny.
Injustice anywhere is a thread to justice
everywhere."

MARTIN LUTHER KING, JR.

UU Service Book #584

K is for Kindness,
>   for care we can give
To all of our neighbors,
>   to help them to live.

KINDNESS You should always expect to find kindness in people of faith, and Unitarian Universalists are particularly good at it — partly because the spirit of our faith is openness, tolerance, and acceptance of each other (our 3rd principle). **UUs do not have dogmas** that separate so-called true believers from others, or worship expectations that force you to come to church under threat of hellfire.

Kindness to others is just an important part of your own life, and of your faith, UUs believe. "You cannot do a kindness too soon," said Emerson, "for you never know how soon it will be too late." Opportunities to show kindness quickly disappear, and your life is the poorer for missing out on **the holy connection to others** that doing a kindness affords. "Kindness is gladdening the hearts of those who are traveling the dark journey with us," said Henri-Frederic Amiel. In other words, kindness "helps them to live."

"We have a great deal more kindness than is
  ever spoken.
The whole human family is bathed with an element
  of love
like a fine ether."

RALPH WALDO EMERSON
UU Service Book #661

L is for Love
and if nothing forbids
It leads to embracing,
to marriage, and kids.

LOVE Love, especially that form of love that we experience as **the emotional attraction to another person**, can be called "the first religion of the earth." It has astonishing power over us, and inclines us to almost worship the one who attracts us. Joy fills the heart in the presence of the one who is loved, and when the loved one turns and loves us in return, the joy becomes much like a religious experience.

The phenomenon is famous in history and literature: lovers sometimes feel transported to another world. The mind and heart is occupied night and day by the joyful thought of our loved one: and "if nothing forbids" (to make it inappropriate), we will link ourselves by sexual intercourse to the other person and produce in each other the physical ecstasy called orgasm, and — in opposite sex couples — possibly fertilization, pregnancy and finally childbirth. No wonder the Bible says "God is love." Same-sex couples experience the same elevation and joy, and make excellent parents through adoption or insemination in various ways. **Homophobia** is a term given to the fear of homosexual love, a phenomenon very seldom encountered in UU congregations.

Many would say that nothing on earth speaks more eloquently of the goodness of creation — or of God — than does the experience of sexual love. There are many other forms of love as well, and all speak eloquently of this as the world's greatest wonder: the magnetism that draws us to each other and to everything we find beautiful.

What an irony it is, then, that sex is often associated with the idea of sin and immorality. Here we come upon a great human challenge: how we can manage our sexual feelings so they are uplifting and not be exploitative. When they become exploitative, we are justly accused of immorality. Abuse of others is always wrong. But reverenced and disciplined, our sexuality can become an important part of our spirituality.

The UU **religious education program for young people** takes up this topic in all its complexity and prepares young people to be their best selves in their use of sexuality all their lives.

> *"Love is not concerned with whom you pray, or where you slept the night you ran away from home. Love is concerned that the beating of your heart should kill no one."*
>
> ALICE WALKER
> UU Service Book #564

M is for Mysteries
    we don't comprehend,
The sweetness of living,
    the tears at the end.

MYSTERIES Mysteries, puzzling and incomprehensible phenomena, are important to UU spirituality. Science is one source of mysteries: how life came about and how it manages to sustain itself on earth in all its innumerable forms. **Science** looks above us to the heavens, at all the awesome speeds and distances of the cosmic bodies, and below us, the microscopic world of mind-boggling complexity and detail through all the elements with their astonishing regularity and breath-taking beauty.

But besides science, philosophy probes other great mysteries: what is knowledge, what might be the purpose of human life, might there be a god whose intelligence and caringness gives meaning to every part of life and death, what makes for beauty in words, in dancing, in music and in every human art, whence the sweetness of living, why the sadness of death.

We live in **a vast cloud of mystery**, and a fascination with these incomprehensible mysteries are part of the UU scene. Many UUs believe in a central mystery called God, but **others are agnostic or atheistic** — but always striving for a reverence for life and the value of human community.

"*Blessed be you, universal matter, unmeasureable time, boundless ether, triple abyss of stars and atoms and generations; You who by overflowing and dissolving our narrow standards of measurement reveal to us the dimensions of God.*"

TEILHARD DE CHARDIN
UU Service Book #549

N is for New,
  for this faith was invented
By people who doubted
  old faiths, and dissented.

NEW   Both Unitarians and Universalists were once liberal Protestant religions, offshoots of Congregationalism. Unitarianism **began as dissent** from Trinitarianism (three persons in God), and Universalism began as dissent from the doctrine that some souls are condemned to eternal hellfire. The two dissenting groups joined forces in 1961.

Today's UUs stand for much more than dissent, of course: for instance we stand for the mutual acceptance of each other, for the valuing of religious pluralism, for all the demanding social idealism of the seven principles. We list among **our heroes** the fourth-century "heretic" Arius, the sixth-century original thinker Origen. Then in the Middle Ages, we honor Michael Servetus — who is often credited with starting this movement with his death at the stake 460 years ago. Soon afterwards Katherine Vogel was similarly martyred for her dissenting beliefs.

Later in the historical line come reformation theologian Francis David and King John Sigismund of Transylvania (the first political figure to allow religious freedom in his realm), and in our own day follow Universalist pastor John Murray and important Unitarians William Ellery Channing and Theodore Parker.

It is not easy to define the UU movement, but one way to think about it is that, instead of being so much a religion in its own right, it is like **a communion of spiritualities**. Whatever may be your spiritual or philosophical approach to life, you are welcome among us.

"Let me not pray to be sheltered from dangers,
But to be fearless in facing them. Let me not
beg for the stilling of my pain, but for the heart
to conquer it."

RABINDRANATH TAGORE
UU Service Book #519

O is for Open,
like minds that have "smarts,"
To see truth in science,
and wisdom in hearts.

OPEN   An open mind is a valued goal for UUs. Among our seven principles we read "acceptance of one another," "a free … search for truth," and "the right of conscience." Like the person with "street smarts," UUs are instinctively suspicious of supernatural revelations since so many of them came from faith traditions which they began to doubt. They generally prefer to keep an open mind, and to depend on intelligent research when truth claims are made. This is sometimes called **"liberal religion"** as opposed to "conservative religion." These two terms have changing meanings very hard to define but the basic difference is that liberals stress freedom of thought, and conservatives stress safeguarding deep values.

Science and the scientific method are highly respected among us also not only as a benefit to humankind but as a discovery of what is awesome in the world. Many famous scientists have been UUs. (See "Famous Unitarians" p. 56.)

"Wisdom in hearts" refers to a kind of knowledge that goes beyond the mind, is informed by the body, by loving relationships, and by wide and deep experience. "The heart has reasons the mind knows nothing of," said Pascal.

The open mind is alert for guidance from all the so-called **wisdom traditions**: Judeo-Christian, Hindu, Buddhist, Taoist, Wiccan, Islamic, and all ancient earth religions.

"I call that mind free which jealously guards its intellectual rights and powers, which does not content itself with a passive or hereditary faith: Which opens itself to light whencesoever it may come; which receives now truth as an angel from heaven."

WILLIAM ELLERY CHANNING
UU Service Book #592

P is for **P**raying,

a way to reflect,

By words or by silence,

then trust, and respect.

PRAYING "Praying" has many meanings. Some UUs pray regularly, some pray not at all: a lot depends on what you mean by praying. Some UU ministers lead the community in prayer, some do not.

Whenever a psalm is read or sung from the hymnal, that is a kind of prayer. Individuals who practice **meditation** may choose to call that prayer. When Americans are surveyed on the subject, a large percentage of them say they pray every day. Ordinary people turn to God in prayer when things go wrong, when tragedy strikes, or when illness comes. There is little harm in this, and often some comfort; but if we think of prayer as "talking to God," then we have lots more to talk about than just our latest need: for instance, gratitude, wonder, fear. See prayers on pages 59 and 61.

Some researchers claim that prayer has a decided effect on the world, others do not find the research convincing. Superstitions abound: certain sets of words are said to have power, certain saints allegedly specialize in particular kinds of miracles, prayers that are long and emotional are said to be effective. The Hebrew Scripture suggests that the works of justice are **the best prayers**. In the Christian Scripture, Jesus advises against long or demonstrative prayers. "Go into your closet and pray," he says. When asked how to pray, Jesus suggested words now known as "The Our Father" or "The Lord's Prayer." But giving God a male name such as "father" is usually considered inadequate, and often "Our Mother" is added, or some other appropriate name.

However we may choose to pray, we do so "with trust" and "with respect." We trust that what we do will be good enough, and we respect the views of others on this subject.

"Prayer cannot bring water to parched land,
nor mend a broken bridge, nor rebuild a ruined city,
but prayer can water an arid soul, mend a broken
heart, and rebuild a weakened will."

ABRAHAM J. HESCHEL
UU Service Book #497

Q is for Questions,
the leaps of the mind,
That move you ahead,
leave your old self behind.

QUESTIONS The wise are constantly questioning. Juan Machado said: "All uncertainty is fruitful ... so long as it is accompanied by the wish to understand." To ask a question is to take a leap with your mind: **scientific inquiry** proceeds on this assumption.

UUs realize that asking a question is their birthright. Some traditional religions discourage questioning. For instance, on the first page of the Koran it states that every word of the book is unquestionably true. **Fundamentalist Christians** also insist that every word of their Bible is accurate, completely true, and guaranteed so by God.

The liberal religious approach is almost opposite to this. Everything about religion and the world is questioned, and one may believe or disbelieve, as long as you search honestly for the truth. "Doubt is part of religion," said John Singer. "All the religious thinkers were doubters." From the Jewish community in Germany in 1939 came the anonymous prayer:

> I believe in the sun
>> even when it is not shining.
> I believe in love
>> even when I do not feel it.
> I believe in God
>> even when God is silent.

"The great end in religious instruction in not to stamp our minds upon the young, but to stir up their own; Not to make them see with our eyes, but to look inquiringly and steadily with their own."

WILLIAM ELLERY CHANNING

UU Service Book #652

R is for **R**everence,
      the awe that we feel
When life seems so sacred,
      it makes our hearts kneel.

REVERENCE "Reverence for life" was the theme of the Unitarian Albert Schweitzer's life and work. The idea struck him unexpectedly, like a mystical experience, and it enabled him to spend his life for the poorest of the poor.

UUs must make **reverence a theme** of their life as well if they are to carry out the seven principles. Reverence demands that we try to see deeply into what is, to feel awe in the presence of mystery, to show respectful hesitation around the great questions, to take time to listen to others and to contemplate the amazing reality around us.

This is what we must teach our children: to respect the web of all existence, to work for world peace, to honor the democratic process, to accept each other's experiences. Sometimes "our hearts kneel" in reverence for all that exists: on the shore of a great ocean, before a sky full of stars.

Ultimately we need not fear reality as it is, but must reverence it. It is essentially the lack of reverence that produced **homophobia**, the fear of same sex affectivity. Homophobic people are not listening reverently to what gay, lesbian, bisexual and transgendered people are saying — which is that they experience genuine love in these relationships. They usually discover themselves not to be straight during puberty. They fall in love with people of their same gender. Not only is there true love between the people involved, but their love is expansive and life-giving, just like the best love experiences of straight people. Our sexuality, whatever it may be, is a blessing, and the source of life's most powerful energies.

"Weave for us a garment of brightness, that we may walk fittingly where birds sing, that we may walk fittingly where grass is green, O our Mother the Earth, O our Father the Sky."

TEWA INDIANS

UU Service Book #520

S is for Spirit,
        unseen, but all-seeing,
A name for the mystery
        beneath all our being.

SPIRIT   On the first page of the Jerusalem Bible, it is said that "God's *spirit*" created everything. "Spirit" in English is the Hebrew word *ruah* which sometimes means breath, sometimes wind, sometimes other things. UUs are **free to believe** that there is and was no such thing, but people of the Abrahamic traditions — Jewish, Moslem, or Christian — usually believe in it.

Like breath, the Spirit is imagined as something unseen, and because it is believed to be divine, it knows everything and is therefore "all-seeing." This Spirit is thought to be immortal and all-compassionate, the force that holds our world together, that designed each creature, that cares infinitely about each living thing, especially ourselves.

This same word "spirit" is used in many other ways: Jesus predicted an era of the Spirit after he was put to death, himself in a spirit form. Divine messengers, **angels**, are often called "spirits," and people who have died are thought by some to remain in existence as spirits. Finally, even the mental and psychological part of a human being is referred to as one's spirit, something unseen but real.

Spirit is a very useful — if inexact — religious word.

"I thank you God for most this amazing
day: for the leaping greenly spirits of trees
and a blue true dream of sky; and for everything
which is natural which is infinite which is yes."

e.e. cummings

UU Service Book #504

T is for Temple,
        some god's habitat,
Though often the cosmos
        itself is like that.

TEMPLE   Where is God? Humans disagree. Some say in "his" temple: that's where God can be found, and so they have built ornate temples (houses for God) all over the earth. On the other extreme those who do believe in a God may claim that **God is everywhere**: since God holds everything in existence minute to minute, God exists everywhere that anything exists. Thus the entire cosmos is God's temple.

Unitarian Universalists — those who are Buddhist, particularly — often tend to be agnostic: they might say "We don't know" anything about any divine personage or group of them. They may say prayers nevertheless. "They speak into the darkness" as theologian Karl Rahner put it, himself a believing Catholic. St. Paul recommends we think of our **bodies as temples** of the spirit, God within, guiding, comforting, empowering.

UUs are encouraged to explore all these opinions. They would not normally call their worship space a "temple." It may look like a church, but sometimes it may look more like a meeting house or a synagogue. What matters is that the people get together there and think about the sacred, sing hymns, and listen to thoughtful sermons.

"In the quietness of this place, surrounded by the all-pervading presence of the Holy, my heart whispers: Keep fresh before me the moments of my High
  Resolve,
that in good times or in tempests, I may not forget that to which my life is committed."

HOWARD THURMAN
UU Service Book #498

U is for Useful,
 the way we should live
To bless those we love
 with the best we can give.

USEFUL A Unitarian Universalist congregation will always try to be a blessing to the people nearby — and those far away as well. Because it follows **a liberal, out-going religious tradition** (not a conservative one mainly intent on conserving values of the past), UUs without hesitation will work to raise money for the needy, help with social causes — like anti-racism, women's rights, and legitimizing same-sex unions — and promote interfaith cooperation.

For UUs there is not — as there is in most other faith communities — any prevailing ideal of personal holiness or evangelism to save souls in some way. If there is any noticeable ideal, it well may be to be useful: useful in fostering democracy and justice, useful in defending the inherent dignity of every person, useful in building peace, education and toleration among people everywhere.

The threat of hellfire and judgment, while commonplace in many religions, comes out of a spirituality based on fear. Many humans are convinced that only if God stands over us, as it were, judging each of our acts — and is ready to punish misbehavior severely — will the human race behave. In Christianity babies are supposedly born in Original Sin, and with minds darkened and wills weakened, standing in the need of "grace" — which the Church gives them access to — to live morally.

Unitarian Universalism has no such negative attitude. It is assumed that children are **born innocent** and full of promise, and have it within their own capacity to live a good, moral life.

"It is today that we fit ourselves for the greater usefulness of tomorrow. Today is the seed time, now are the hours of work, and tomorrow comes the harvest and the playtime."

W.E.B. DUBOIS

UU Service Book #502

V is for Vision,

　　　　when leaders reveal

How their fresh ideas

　　　make future dreams real.

VISION   "Without vision, the nation perishes," says the Hebrew scripture. Democracy is of visionary import in UUism. Local church leaders are elected by the members. National UU leaders are chosen democratically also, and the process includes election campaigns in which potential leaders explain their vision to others and try to win their votes. National meetings called **"General Assembly"** are held annually in some North American city, and there delegates from each congregation (about 1000 of these in the U.S.) vote on improvements to official policies.

The UU vision for a better world also embraces freedom of religious expression, respect for reason and conscience, equality of the sexes, opportunity for education and work for all, societal care for everyone in need, and the inclusion of all of creation in a healthy web of life on earth with respect for **animal rights** as well. Once a member decides to be part of that vision, s/he "signs the book" and officially belongs, taking on some responsibility for the church including its financial needs. Each year a "canvass" asks members to pledge their fair share of the financial burdens of both their own community and of the national and international movement. It is a thrilling vision to be part of. Perhaps the UU style may even be a useful communitarian model for the whole world's religious future.

"There is deep power in which we exist and whose beatitude is accessible to us. Each moment when the individual feels invaded by it — is memorable."

RALPH WALDO EMERSON

UU Service Book #531

W is for Working. . .
at building the earth —
When people of faith see
how great is its worth.

WORKING It takes a kind of faith to appreciate where we humans live: on a planet with limited resources — spinning through space around a burning star. Earth is our space ship, and scientists tell us that the people on the space ship **are ruining its life-giving resources**: the air, the water, and the soil. It takes extraordinary faith — and reflectiveness — to want to help save our space vehicle because all around us people live in the illusion that earth's resources are endless, its air super-plentiful, and its oceans infinite.

That is not the attitude of Unitarian Universalists. UUs in 1995 added to their list of sources of spiritual teaching "earth-centered traditions" — which honor our planet as holy and worthy of ultimate respect. A few years earlier the UUs added as a seventh foundational principle "respect for **the interdependent web** of all existence of which we are a part."

Author Forrest Church puts this first. He writes: "Our denomination's sixth source ... holds a primary place in our faith's typology. A sense of the earth as a touchstone of the sacred, indeed as holy ground, comes before Judaism and Christianity, before the other world religions, before all the philosophers of humanism." Deep caringness for earth's environment is a specialty for Unitarian Universalists.

"From making war and calling it peace, special
  privilege
and calling it justice, indifference and calling it
  tolerance,
pollution and calling it progress, may we be cured."

HARRY MESERVE

UU Service Book #496

X is for **X**-rays

that science designed

For looking at bones —

but not spirit, or mind.

X-RAYS X-rays are a source of information that is not available on the surface of things. They "look within," yet cannot see the human spirit or the human mind. There are other ways of studying spirit and mind, and UUs have named six so-called "sources of our faith."

1. Direct experience of **that transcending mystery** and wonder, affirmed in all cultures, which moves us to a renewal of the spirit and an openness to the forces that create and uphold life;
2. Words and deeds of prophetic women and men, which challenge us to confront powers and structures of evil with justice, compassion, and the transforming power of love;
3. **Wisdom from the world's religions**, which inspires us in our ethical and spiritual life;
4. Jewish and Christian teachings, which call us to respond to God's love by loving our neighbors as ourselves;
5. Humanist teachings, which counsel us to heed the guidance of reason and the findings of science;
6. Spiritual teachings of earth-centered traditions, which celebrate the sacred circle of life and instruct us to live in harmony with the rhythms of nature.

From these rich sources comes the UU religion, an empowering and liberating faith tradition.

"Thou art the path and the goals that paths never reach. Thou feedest and sustainest all that one sees, or seems. Thou art the light in sun and moon, the sounds fading into silence, and the sanctity of sacred books."

PRAYER FROM INDIA

UU Service Book #523

Y is for Youthful,
when vigor is new
Though sometimes old people
can be youthful too.

YOUTHFUL   The UU faith is itself youthful, the Universalist tradition establishing its first American church only in 1779, the Unitarian's first church set up in 1787. They joined forces in 1961.

Also, young people often take to the UU tradition with enthusiasm since the atmosphere is so open, and their youthful opinions are taken so seriously.

In addition, there is an inherent sense of youthfulness for all members in belonging to **a fast-growing religious movement**. Change is always in the air as the UU impulse toward inclusion, pluralism and toleration takes an interest in every religious and ethical issue that is alive in our times.

Even our religious education of children emphasizes openness to all religious traditions. From their earliest years UU children are encouraged to formulate their own personal beliefs and moral values. We do not insist on a belief in an Original Sin (inherited from Adam and Eve) or in the necessity of a washing, a "baptism" to remove it. Instead children are **officially "dedicated"** to the liberal traditions of the faith because their parents are convinced of their beauty and importance.

The dedication ceremony is not fixed and official, but simply presents the child to the community as a blessing for all, congratulates the parents, and welcomes the child into the care of everyone.

"If we are to reach real peace in this world,
and if we are to carry on a real war against war,
we shall have to begin with the children.
It is possible to live in peace. The future depends
on what we do in the present."

MOHANDAS K. GANDHI

UU Service Book #577

Z is for **Z**ero —

    when everything's gone:

Some say that is sunset,

    but some say it's dawn.

ZERO Zero is a mathematical concept but it may be considered as a metaphor, **a symbol, of death**. In death, everything's gone, it seems: the life of your body, the liveliness of your mind and your ability to communicate. You become a zero, as it were.

Or do you? Many people would say that perhaps you go on living somehow, your personality changing into something un-bodily — a spirit — joining in some great fellowship made up of all who have lived a mortal life on earth, now becoming perhaps immortal, experiencing the dawn of a new life, *adding* a zero, as it were, to the sum total of what you were on earth. It is possible. "Nothing is too wonderful to exist," said scientist Michael Faraday. The world is already full of similar, almost unbelievable wonders.

Death is a great mystery, an unknown. Next to the awesomeness of birth, death is deeply awesome in its terrible unknowns, and its sadness, and its possibilities. **UUs range in opinion** about all this from total disbelief to agnosticism to complete faith. Forrest Church, for instance, states that life after death is "a possibility little more remote than that there should be life in the first place."

But no one's opinion is discounted or officially endorsed, and that adds to the bracing atmosphere of open-mindedness and searching that makes the UU faith so attractive.

"Sorrow will one day turn to joy. All that breaks the heart and oppresses the soul will one day give place to peace and understanding and everyone will be free."

PAUL ROBESON
UU Service Book #689

Famous People in the UU Movement

John Adams	U.S. President
John Quincy Adams	U.S. President
Horatio Alger	Author
Conrad Aiken	Poet and novelist
Louisa May Alcott	Author
Susan B. Anthony	Activist for women's right to vote
P.T. Barnum	Showman
Béla Bartók	Composer
Alexander Graham Bell	Scientist, inventor of the telephone
Olympia Brown	First woman minister in U.S.
Luther Burbank	Scientist
Robert Burns	Poet
Rachel Carson	Author
William Ellery Channing	Abolitionist, founder of Unitarianism
ee cummings	Poet
Charles Darwin	Scientist, Evolutionist
Charles Dickens	Novelist
Ralph Waldo Emerson	Author, philosopher, Unitarian minister
Fanny Farmer	Cookbook author
Millard Fillmore	U.S. President
Robert Fulghum	Author
Ben Franklin	Scientist, author, statesman
Horace Greeley	Journalist, politician
Nathaniel Hawthorne	Author
Oliver Wendell Holmes	Author, U.S. Supreme Court Justice
Julia Ward Howe	Composer, activist

Thomas Jefferson	Philosopher, U.S. President
Henry Wadsworth Longfellow	Poet
Amy Lowell	Poet, abolitionist, minister
Herman Melville	Author
Samuel Morse	Scientist, inventor of the telegraph
Paul Newman	Movie star
Thomas Paine	Patriot, editor
Theodore Parker	Abolitionist, author
Linus Pauling	Nobel Prize-winning chemist
Sylvia Plath	Author
Beatrix Potter	Author
Joseph Priestley	Scientist, minister, discoverer of oxygen
Paul Revere	Patriot
Carl Sandberg	Pulitzer Prize-winning poet
Margaret Sanger	Activist for birth control
Albert Schweitzer	Author, medical missionary
Adlai Stevenson	Governor of Illinois, presidential candidate
William Taft	U.S. President
Kurt Vonnegut	Author
Daniel Webster	Orator, presidential candidate
Frank Lloyd Wright	Architect
Whitney Young	Head of the Urban League

More information at www.famoususs.com and www.uuwhs.org.

Interfaith Prayers

MORNING BLESSING God of all that is, your servant stands ready for another day. I thank you for your gift of life, for consciousness, and for hope. With your blessing my lively heart will beat on today. May it be compassionate and serve your purposes so that, at nightfall, I can lie down in peace of mind, safe in your loving care. Amen.

EVENING BLESSING All-Compassionate God, I rest now in your blessing, however the day may have been, however may be my future. It is an honor to be a part of this evolving creation and I thank you for being my Companion in everything. As much as possible I forgive my enemies, hoping to be forgiven all my own faults. With peace of soul I entrust myself into your hands. Amen.

GRACE BEFORE MEALS God of Life, we thank you for each hand that helped put food before us, for the taste we enjoy from mother earth, for the nourishment and energy that comes to us from nature, and for the communion with others it all provides. Amen.

PRAYER IN DISTRESS Loving God, you know our pain and sorrow in all its trying details. Be with us, Holy Mystery, you who can bring meaning and rebirth out of absurdity and defeat. We surrender to the mysterious way of your creation, and honor your merciful presence everywhere among us. Amen.

DAILY BLESSING O God, you are truly a father to us as you are our mother. We thank you for your strength and goodness, God our Father. And we thank you for your kindly caring, God our mother. Holy Mystery, we thank you for the great love you have for each one of us. Amen. (Julian of Norwich)

PRAYER FOR HEALING Holy God of this evolving world, we put all our troubles into your hands. May goodness come of this trying affliction, and an ennobling strength from this human challenge. We believe your heart is on our side, and your holy presence here to bless us in every way you can. Amen.

Prayers from World Religions

BUDDHIST Attend to this very day: it is life, the truest life of your life. In its brief course lie many mysteries: bliss is one, the splendor of beauty is another. Yesterday is but a dream, tomorrow is only a vision, but this day well spent makes every yesterday a happy dream and every tomorrow a hopeful vision. Attend to this very day: it is life.

MOSLEM I love, O God, the scent of the air, straight from your inner courts, the perfumed garments of the garden healing us all. I join the trees in their worship, the birds in their praise, the new blue violets in their surrender.

HINDU O God, enemy of folly and ignorance, grant me the joy that all beings may see me with the eye of a friend, and that I may see all beings with the eye of a friend, and that all beings see all beings with the eye of a friend.

NATIVE AMERICAN Grandfather God, behold our brokenness. In all creation only the human family has strayed from the Sacred Way. We are divided and do not walk together on the Sacred Way. Holy One, teach us love, compassion and honor that we may heal the earth and heal each other.

ASHANTI O God, creator of our homeland, earth, trees, animals and humans – all that is – honors you. Drums beat out our worship, people sing it and dance with noisy pleasure: You are God, You are God, You are God.

SHINTO Before the great Parent God I speak with reverence, and pray that I may not be taken hold of by narrow desires but show forth the divine generosity by living a life of wide creativity – growing from an authentic self.

Afterword

HOW THIS BOOK CAME TO BE

It was in Seneca Falls, N.Y., at the Women's Rights Museum, that I found on display what must be a famous old fashioned children's book, all about the abolition of slavery but organized by A, B, C's, an old fashioned kind of children's book called an abecedary. It was probably written before 1860, and was placed in the museum because of its memorable success as a book used by women to instruct their children in social justice.

It electrified me.

The book itself was almost square, and when you opened it to page one, you could see on the left panel, the giant A, then on the book's right panel, the giant B.

Each letter of the alphabet was followed by a rhyming verse, and the whole book carried you — in rhyme and in striking graphics on every page — through the topic of slavery and abolition, giving the person reading to the child an opportunity to discuss and explain the morality (the immorality, really) of the topic. A child would instantly understand through the graphics what the book was about. A parent would then read the rhyming couplets and explain them.

My thought: why not do this for Unitarian Universalism?

So I did. I began with the children's book project (to be called *My UU ABCs*), then added this companion for parents, *The ABCs for UU Newcomers*. With the help of the Women's Alliance of our church (to whom I owe great thanks), we are launching this adult book first — after testing it with our own newcomers.

My hope is our book will achieve some of the usefulness of its famous model.

William Cleary
Fall 2002

William Cleary
72A North Prospect Street
Burlington, Vermont 05401
802-862-4659
bcleary412@aol.com
www.clearyworks.com